This book is dedicated to all who find Nature not an adversary to conquer and destroy, but a storehouse of infinite knowledge and experience linking man to all things past and present. They know conserving the natural environment is essential to our future well-being.

GRAND STAIRCASE-ESCALANTE

THE STORY BEHIND THE SCENERY®

by Joyce Badgley Hunsaker

JOYCE BADGLEY HUNSAKER is a nationally acclaimed author whose works about the American West have been featured in such respected forums as the Smithsonian Institution and TIME magazine. She lost her heart to the Grand Staircase country three decades ago, and today lives at its gateway in Kanab.

JOHN P. GEORGE fell in love with exploring and photographing Southern Utah's Redrock canyons and mesas 32 years ago. The passion continues stronger than ever. He also ventures throughout the National Parks and wilderness areas, in search of primal beauty.

Grand Staircase - Escalante National Monument, located in Southern Utah, was created by Presidential Proclamation in 1996 to protect this remarkable landscape's vast array of scientific and historic resources.

Front cover: Slick Rock Mesas, Inside front cover: Flat Top Rock, Page 1: Mule deer, Pages 2/3: Aquarius Plateau, photos by John P. George.

Edited by Maryellen Conner. Book design by K. C. DenDooven.

Autumnal shadows accentuate mysteries of the Escalante Canyon's northern boundary along the Aquarius Plateau. Consistent with the

constellation which lends its name to the area, water is
the wizard here, transforming naked sandstone into
life-supporting grasses, ferns, flowering plants, shrubs, and trees.

The Grand Staircase—Escalante Story

Pinnacles of eroded Navajo
Sandstone—hoodoos—jut from
bases of petrified sand dunes laid down some 200 million
years ago. Part of the Grand Staircase's White Cliffs "step",
this sandstone's characteristic pale ivories, tans, and soft
reddish-browns flush golden at sunrise, accentuating
its distinctive cross-bedded structure.

Most first-time visitors to Grand Staircase-Escalante National Monument ask simply, "Where's the staircase?" Perhaps they envision a natural stone structure they can scale on a day hike. Maybe some expect an impressive man-constructed ascent like those found at well-known temple ruins such as Tikal, Chichen Itza, or Machu Picchu.

Few are prepared for what they actually see: an unbroken series of gargantuan, technicolored terraces and cliffs covering over 1,000 square miles (2,600 square kilometers) of the Colorado Plateau, thrusting nearly a mile in relief from bottom "step" to top, and exposing over 200 million years of layered geologic history in their ascent. The Chocolate Cliffs, the Vermilion Cliffs, the White Cliffs, Gray Cliffs, and finally—the highest step in this stairway to the sky—the Pink Cliffs. Here is the Grand Staircase!

The Staircase itself is only the western-most third of the monument which bears its name. Nearly two million acres of almost incomprehensible variety and complexity (that's over 2900 square miles/7,540 square kilometers) comprise the Bureau of Land Management's Grand Staircase-Escalante National Monument overall. The Kaiparowits Plateau and the Escalante Canyons—each a distinctive system of geology, biology, and human culture, divided by the equally distinctive Cockscomb and Straight Cliffs—make up the remaining two-thirds of this isolated region which

The unforgettable jagged, upended ridge of the Cockscomb stands sentry between the Grand Staircase and extraordinarily fossil-rich Kaiparowits Plateau regions of the Monument. Geologically known as the East Kaibab Monocline, the Cockscomb snakes from the Colorado River through Cottonwood Canyon to Highway 12. Faulting, flexing, and folding of the earth's crust created its peculiar shapes. Poet and painter Maynard Dixon likened the Cockscomb to a massive protruding skeleton. Others perceived sharp teeth of a gigantic saw blade, or a rooster's serrated crown. Some, in the early days, simply called it "Gateway to No Man's Land." Powerful landscape elicits powerful emotional response. What are you feeling here?

was the last place in the continental United States to be mapped.

Bordered by Bryce Canyon National Park to the northwest, Capitol Reef National Park to the northeast, and Glen Canyon National Recreation Area and Lake Powell to the east and south, this spectacular region is a feast for eye and imagination. Whether examined from the perspective of science or recreation opportunities, Grand Staircase Escalante National Monument is a true frontier of knowledge and discovery.

TOM DANIELSEN

The story of the Escalante Canyons is one written by water: rain, snow, streams, waterfalls, flash floods. From sinuous slot canyons to scattered benches of tillable soil and timbered mountain slopes, abundance of water here is key.

*F*or this unforgiving yet seductive land,
stripped by millennia to its barest essentials,
water truly is its lifeblood. In many places,
the Monument feels like the remnant of
a different planet. And in a sense, it is!

Where the West Stays Wild

Modern sculptors chisel away stone encasing their intended designs, eventually "liberating" the finished pieces from their host material. Sunset Arch formed in much the same way as softer rock weathered away from harder, creating this window to the Straight Cliffs and Navajo Mountain.

The Circle Cliffs' arresting shapes, textures, and colors testify to a long-vanished oil and gas reservoir here. The high rock "crown" surrounding this area's deeply eroded center tells of a dome whose fracture freed the trapped oil and gases millions of years ago.

As the largest National Monument in the continental United States, distances here are commonly measured in the number of hours, days, or weeks, "sleeps" or "looks"—required to traverse it, rather than surface miles. To experience the Monument most fully, one should employ the eye of an artist, the soul of a poet, the intellectual curiosity of a scientist, and the stamina of an athlete.

In truth, Grand Staircase-Escalante National Monument is a great dragon of a land where the bones of the earth are laid bare. It is a land filled with strange wind- and water-carved shapes bearing even stranger names that make today's human beings feel alien: hoodoos, rock rainbows, alcoves and arches, pinnacles and spires, slot canyons, comb ridges, cross-bedded bluffs, checkerboarded mesas. Add to these: sculpted slickrocks, fossilized sand dunes, crumbling badlands, and dry rock puddles brimming with round iron balls called "moqui marbles." The land's isolation has preserved its uniqueness... and its wonder.

Water
is BOTH
the *great*
creator and
destroyer....
The *SOURCE* of
All possibility

***T**he shimmering ribbon of Lower Calf Creek Falls flows* *year-round, bringing life and continuous change to the stone amphitheater into which it flows. A day hike favored by visitors for its scenic beauty, the falls and its pool also draw an array of wildlife from the Escalante Canyons region for sustenance.*

Often termed simply "red rock country" due to the dominant color of its rusting, iron-saturated sandstones, the landscape's palette actually reveals an astonishing variety of oxidizing, mineralized hues. Rich burgundies, velvety browns, and deep purple-blacks spill over soft oranges, blood-bright crimsons, and shocking vermilions. Salmons, ambers, and ivories ribbon in and out of formations pigmented peach, apricot, lavender-blue, and grey. Each color represents a distinct chemical composition. Each gives clues about how fluids have flowed over or through landforms in the past... and how they flow through now. In this country every color, every wind-pushed particle, has a story to tell.

Where there is water, there is green: exuberant, variegated, living green. You touch it in the mossy tendrils of Calf Creek Falls in the Escalante Canyons. You smell it in the spongy, dripping seeps of Hackberry Canyon, west of the Cockscomb. You marvel at its tenacity in the natural tinajas, or water-gathering holes, of the slickrock country anchored by juniper and pinyon pine... then again in the isolated fingers of tillable benches and leveled slumps, so highly prized by the Ancestral Puebloans and pioneering homesteaders.

For this unforgiving yet seductive land, stripped by millennia to its barest essentials, water truly is its lifeblood. Whether in the form of seasonal rains, high-country snowpacks, unexpected cloudbursts or roiling flash floods, water is both Great Creator and Destroyer, the source of all possibility.

Rivers flow red when they capture a super-saturation of red sandstone particles washed down from the rocks. Flash floods both scour out river channels, and deposit new layers of rock and soil upon which vegetation can take hold and thrive.

CLUES TO OUR PLANET'S MYSTERIOUS PAST

In many places, the Monument feels like the remnant of a different planet. And in a sense, it is. Most of the geologic formations here contain fossils. Together the rocks and fossils, remnants of an environment far different from the one we inhabit now, form a valuable and fascinating library of clues covering almost 270 million years of Earth's history.

The oldest exposed rocks (from the Paleozoic Era) tell of the equator cutting across the southeast corner of today's Utah. They testify to ancient seas encroaching upon—then receding from—marine lowlands, flood plains, and tidal flats... progressively laying down shell, coral, and sponge-filled limestone between red beds of sandstone and mudstone on adjacent lowlands.

As millennia passed, additional deposits of sand, gravel, soils, silts, and organics settled into many distinct sedimentary layers covering the area. Continents moved. Earth's crust compressed, buckled, broke open. Mountains jutted up. Volcanoes spewed. Inland seas finally retreated.

Globally, climates fluctuated many times. Magnetic poles reversed. Locally, sand dunes over a thousand feet tall drifted over one another and compacted together. Populations of exotic life forms flourished and fell, or became extinct. Others rose to take their places. The only constant, scientifically speaking, was—and still is—change.

Fortunately, change leaves evidence in its wake. Some evidence is so minute, it cannot be detected with the naked eye. Some evidence is spectacular, such as the second largest fossil forest in North America—from the beginning of the Age of Dinosaurs, some 225 million years ago—discovered within the Circle Cliffs of the Escalante Canyons. There are dinosaur bones, teeth, tendons, tail-drags, and tracks—even dinosaur skin "mummies"—eroding daily out of wind-scoured hollows and ancient streambeds of the Kaiparowits Plateau. (See pages 40-41, for rare photographs.) The sequence of rocks displayed here contains one of the best and most complete records of Late Cretaceous terrestrial life (95 to 65 million years ago) found anywhere in the world.

*A*ncient cousins of this collared lizard skittered, swayed, and lumbered across mud flats of shrinking stream beds and inland seas. The dramas of their daily lives became encoded in that mud: footprints, tail drags, wallows, skirmishes, even death. Mud became stone. Today, those stones speak through fossil evidence to help us better understand our natural world — past, present, and maybe future.

Paleontologists have discovered many fossils on the Kaiparowits of unique and sometimes unknown species: dinosaurs, marine reptiles, birds, lizards, giant crocodiles, turtles, amphibians, invertebrates, plants and trees. They have even unearthed rare, fossilized Late Cretaceous mammal teeth and tracks. These provide tantalizing glimpses into ancient ecosystems as the Age of Dinosaurs catapulted into the Rise of Mammals.

Different evidence is found where coal seams snake deep inside the earth's crust. The seams, themselves, are the fossils; remnants of a time when subtropical vegetation flourished in warm coastal swamps. Ignited at the surface by lightning, they have smoldered for tens of thousands of years. At times, they billow grey smoke skyward, giving Smoky Mountain Road its name. Atop the Burning Hills, they still scorch rocks into brick-red clinkers.

Grand Staircase-Escalante National Monument is far from static. Instead, this "last frontier" is a dynamic landscape bridging past and present; a timescape of intimate connectedness.

Or, as tribal peoples of this region say, "Everything is related. It is all One."

SUGGESTED READING

Fleischner, Thomas Lowe, *Singing Stone.* Salt Lake City, Utah: The University of Utah Press, 1999.

Ladd, Gary, *Landforms of the Colorado Plateau: The Story Behind the Scenery.* Las Vegas, Nevada: KC Publications, Inc., 1998.

Sprinkel, Douglas A., Chidsey, Thomas C., and Anderson, Paul B., ed., *Geology of Utah's Parks and Monuments.* Salt Lake City, Utah: Utah Geological Association, 2003.

At *Devil's Garden, off Hole-In-The-Rock Road,*
Mother Nature has carved Entrada Sandstone
into dramatic freeform goblins, monoliths, and gravity-defying spans such as Metate Arch. Behind the
arch – midway down the ivory-colored layer—a second, smaller, arch is beginning. The Monument's
landscape is a work in progress, an unceasing process of tearing down and building up.

K.C. DENDOOVEN

Grand Staircase

The broad staircased swath comprising the far western third of the Monument is a series of distinctive gargantuan benches and cliffs that progressively step up in elevation from south to north. The bottom of the staircase correlates with the highest bench of the Grand Canyon; the topmost riser, with the signature spires of Bryce Canyon. These massive layers of multi-hued shales, sandstones, and limestones span over 200 million years of geologic history. Their variation in altitude and precipitation has produced three distinct zones of climate—desert, semi-desert, and upland—with corresponding distinctive flora, fauna, and human culture. The Grand Staircase is a treasure trove of unforgettable artistic vistas, exciting scientific possibilities, and almost-overwhelming sensory experiences in any season.

Water erodes harder rock in sharper, narrower slices than it does softer, less resistant, rock. Slot canyons are formed by this continuous slicing action along major fractures, accelerated by seasonal flash flooding which abrades the canyon walls with tons of water, sand, rock fragments and organics moving at incredibly high speeds.

Earth's crust buckled, bent, folded, and ultimately stood on end to form the unforgettable shapes of the Cockscomb. In places the ridge appears to be turned upside down and inside out, thanks to the dynamics which created it. Erosion has only accentuated its strangeness, wearing away the colorful Carmel and Entrada sediments at differing rates and angles.... leaving behind an ever-changing masterpiece.

As rock wears down around Deer Springs Point, stabilizing grasses, plants, shrubs, and trees move in. Native peoples developed uses for many of these: food, medicines, building materials, clothing, dyes. Pioneers later adopted some of these uses and discovered new ones of their own.

JERRY SINTZ

Over three hundred movies and TV shows – many of them classic westerns – have been filmed on lands now encompassed by the Monument. Portions of the film sets, such as those from Gunsmoke and The Outlaw Josie Wales, still exist.

KC DENDOOVEN

Forming the easternmost boundary of the Kaiparowits Plateau, the Straight Cliffs are actually a fifty-mile escarpment of stacked marine sandstone—ancient beach sand! Ninety million years ago, lush swamps formed behind these sandstone layers, giving rise to the coal seams frequently seen throughout the Kaiparowits.

Kaiparowits Plateau

In the central portion of the Monument lies the Kaiparowits Plateau. Covering about 1,650 square miles (2,655 square kilometers), the Kaiparowits is bounded on the west by the spectacularly jagged Cockscomb ridge and on the east by the wild and imposing Straight Cliffs, sometimes called Fifty Mile Mountain. In the early days, settlers most often referred to this breathtakingly desolate and inhospitable region as "No Man's Land." True, in many places it still has the weird starkness of a moonscape. But to scientists, this is paleo-central. The Jurassic and Cretaceous sandstones of the Kaiparowits Plateau have yielded a mind-boggling array of fossils, some of them new to science. One of the world's best and most complete records of terrestrial life 95 - 65 million years ago (Late Cretaceous Period), is being uncovered daily here.

JOYCE HUNSAKER

Steaming vents along Smoky Mountain Road belch gases bearing the strong smells of creosote and tar. Underground coal fires here and throughout the Burning Hills have been smoldering for centuries.

As its name implies, the hard capstone balanced atop this pillar protects the under-rocks from weathering. Iron particles which color the sandstone red also help cement it, making it less susceptible to erosion than the crumbling white base layer. Eventually, however, Mother Nature will take her toll and this pillar will collapse. The capstone will topple and come to rest on another patch of rock or soil to protect it, thus beginning the process anew.

Escalante Canyons

The Escalante Canyons are a massive network of steep, brilliantly-colored narrow canyons and great rounded slickrock jumbles sculpted by the Escalante River drainage. This very popular, scenic eastern third of the Monument is bounded on the north by Boulder Mountain and the Aquarius Plateau, on the east by Waterpocket Fold, and on the south by the Colorado River's Glen Canyon. The names are not accidental. Abundance of water is key in the Escalante Canyons, giving rise to an astonishing diversity of flora, fauna, and intriguing landforms. Its history of human habitation is long and varied, including ancient tribal sites and later, those of newer tribes, pioneers and settlers. This region also contains one of the largest fossil forests in North America.

Wolverine Petrified Forest is scattered with large sections of 225-million-year-old petrified logs, stumps, and limbs from now-extinct conifer trees. One uncovered tree trunk measures six feet in diameter and is nearly 90 feet long!

LIN ALDER

Long Canyon beckons to a trip through time, through emotion, through an artist's palette. Colossal, towering rockfaces hug the highway on either side, creating a surreal "slot canyon" experience for cars. The beauty is so intense here, you will have to remind yourself to breathe.

Navajo sandstone comes in many colors, but sometimes fluids flush through the rock and bleach away the iron, leaving behind the original color of sand. This iron precipitates concretions and deposits with weird shapes, including perfectly round spheres locally called Moqui Marbles.

Double arches inside Peek-A-Boo slot canyon provide amazing portals into an ancient world. Two hundred million years ago, during the Mesozoic Era, one of the largest deserts ever known on earth existed here. Some of the structures in the sandstone tell us dunes were up to a thousand feet high and pushed by winds so strong, some of the sand particles actually originated in the Appalachian Mountains – more than half a continent away!

Even little rodents known as "pack rats"
give scientists insight as to what species
have existed in the past
that might not be prevalent now.

All Things are Connected

Because the Monument's scale is so massive and vast, it's easy to almost overlook the smaller miracles waiting at every turn. But even the tiniest element of the natural world—or lack of it—can make a huge difference in the "big picture."

Two-legged, four-legged, no-legged, finned, feathered, or scaled, all life in the desert is dependent upon water to survive. The Monument is home to more than 200 bird species, 25 amphibian and reptile species, a host of fishes, over 100 mammal species, 1600 insect and invertebrate species, plus nearly 1000 species of plants.

Even the satiny brown-black stain decorating canyon walls and cliff faces—called "desert varnish"—is actually alive. Water dripping over and through the sandstone rocks for millennia has created a veneer of dust and clay, cemented in place by living bacteria and microfungi. The varnish, in turn, provides a fertile birthing ground for specialized lichens and algae.

Some life forms found on the Monument—such as the California condor, Kodachrome bladderpod, the Colorado pike minnow, and others—are listed as threatened or endangered.

Water seeps follow fractures along a cliff face, gently eroding underlying rock until alcoves form. Protected from wind and sun, moisture-loving plants like these maidenhair ferns thrive in what becomes a hanging garden. This microhabitat encourages other ferns, mosses, flowers, and grasses which couldn't survive elsewhere. Seeps also provide ready water sources for birds, animals, insects, bats...and humans.

Millennia of moisture-borne minerals sluicing over and through this sentinel of Horse Canyon have created its cloak of desert varnish. Bacteria and microfungi, smaller than a single human red blood cell, colonize on sunblasted rockfaces to produce these living veneers. Early native peoples especially favored such surfaces for incising their petroglyphs.

TOM DANIELSEN

Some are completely new to science, found nowhere else in the world.

Others have evolved to thrive in only very specific environments. Certain amphibians, for instance, can lie dormant in the ground for decades until just the right amount of water saturates their "sanctuary", signaling conditions will sustain them above ground. Certain seeds require abrasion to germinate—brushing against rock or sand, or being handled by small mammals.

Since the Monument covers five full life-zones within its borders, vegetation—hence, life that is dependent upon it—may vary widely from place to place. Elevation, temperature, soil composition or compaction, and especially water (or lack of it) determine whether four-wing saltbush will grow in a certain location, or Utah serviceberry, or ponderosa pine, and whether the whiptail lizard makes its home there, the mountain lion, or American black bear.

"this LAND is Alive"

say the tribal people

"It GETS into your blood"

say the descendants of pioneers

Both sagebrush and yellow-flowering snakeweed were used medicinally by native peoples and settlers in the early days. Some tribes still use them ceremonially. Wildlife sometimes use their buds and seeds as a food source. Today scientists consider the sagebrush – icon of the cowboy way of life – an important indicator of rangeland health. Drought, overgrazing, and soil compaction by hoof- , foot-, and tire-traffic all impact sage growth and distribution.

Of the 500 bee species so far identified on the Monument, some pollinate only certain kinds—or colors—of plants. Certain species visit only cactus blossoms. The black andrena bee collects pollen solely from the evening primrose...and only at dawn before temperature, light, and changed humidity cause the flower to close. Without this reciprocity, many plants wouldn't be able to blossom or produce seeds which, in turn, provide a main source of food for wildlife.

Animals, too, play an important role by distributing seeds in their droppings or storage caches, or carrying seeds in their hair and fur. Any hiker who has bent to pick sharp cheat grass "tips" out of his socks, has experienced first-hand how effective this distribution technique is.

This region's diversity has demanded adaptation and specialization. When those demands have become too many—or too drastic—in too short a time, entire species have vanished.

TURNING BACK THE CLOCK

One of the Monument's mandates is to achieve a natural range of native (or "endemic") plants and animals. In some cases, this means that certain absent species—such as pronghorn and desert bighorn sheep—should be re-introduced, while some invasive, non-native species—such as cheat grass or tamarisk—must be closely contained or eradicated.

But how do we know what those native species were?

The kangaroo rat is well-suited for desert life with sharp teeth that can strip bark and shred seed coverings. Powerful back legs help this little gatherer stand upright and hop big distances in little time.

Omnivorous but fastidious eaters, raccoons like to wash wherever water is present. Perhaps these mud-prints will become fossils to fascinate tomorrow's paleontologists!

Fortunately, some parts of the Monument are so remote and inaccessible to casual traffic, they remain little changed and unmodified. These can be used by scientists as "base samples" to help show what species are native to the region, and in what conditions they thrive.

For other areas that have supported human occupation or transit, the prehistoric and historic records are consulted. Pictographs, petroglyphs, plant and animal remains found in archaeological sites all provide vital clues, as do traditional tribal stories and ceremonies, pioneer diaries, and explorers' and surveyors' journals.

Even little rodents known as "pack rats" give scientists insight as to what species have existed in the past that might not be prevalent now. Infamous for their habit of gathering and hoarding bits of this and that, pack rats build up mounds of debris at the bases of dead trees or cacti, or in rock crevices, to cover their nests. These nests can be occupied continuously for hundreds—even thousands—of years by generations of pack rats. Every scrap they gather gets glued together by urine and droppings, which preserves them in a viscous glaze. When studied by scientists, these accumulated bits of bone, seeds, hair, and plant parts can help decipher past climatic conditions, animal ranges, and vegetation patterns... in some places, up to 25,000 years ago!

Beautiful prickly pear cactus blossoms advertise pollen to a variety of insects. Its spines can be employed (carefully!) as fasteners or awls. The pads can be boiled for poultices, the inner flesh and seeds roasted for food.

Biological crusts have carpeted vast sections of the Colorado Plateau for tens of thousands of years. Like these off Skutumpah Road, they have protected the soil against erosion and have provided viable conditions for seeds to take hold. They have increased water absorption, glued soil particles together, and added essential nutrients for soil fertility. With increased disturbance by human habitation and transit, however, the loss of these cryptobiotic soils—with subsequent erosion and soil depletion—is rapidly changing the nature of the entire ecosystem: plants, wildlife, water tables, soils. Healthy, undisturbed crusts are essential to a sustainable environment.

INTERDEPENDENCY

At first glance, the desert may appear to be barren or sterile. While it is true that rivers, pools, and seeps support most of the landscape's obvious life, you may be surprised at what you find when you just look closer.

What is that lumpy, bumpy, crunchy stuff that covers so much of the ground visitors encounter on the Monument?

That's biological soil crust, or *cryptobiotic* soil, and it is very much alive. True to its name (crypto = hidden; bios = life), this is a thriving community of

Temperature fluctuations and erosion have hollowed out sandstone depressions Spanish explorers dubbed "tinajas" (tin-AH-hahs), or "little water jars". These shallow pools seasonally fill with snow or rain, providing welcome watering holes for wildlife. Then, as temperatures warm, tinajas teem with aquatic and insect life. They eventually dry, leaving behind a crusted "bathtub ring" until the next cycle.

lichens, algae, mosses and microfungi. Its purpose is to trap rock and sand particles in a protective, nutrient rich mantle suitable for plant growth. Cyanobacteria within the crust produce thin, sticky filaments that bind these particles together creating an erosion-resistant, sponge-like "shell". They capture air and water-borne elements (nitrogen, calcium, potassium, etc.) which, in turn, they convert into fertilizer. Then, these crusts snare seeds.

Though not as immediately impressive, perhaps, as a rock arch or hoodoo, soil crusts are much more important, for they provide stability, nutrients, and moisture to environments that otherwise could not sustain life. Stepping on a well-developed patch can destroy decades of growth, and leave loose undersoil exposed to erosion and degradation. Full recovery can take up to several centuries, so appreciate—and respect—this basic building block of life in the desert.

CONNECTIONS

Though at first the grandeur of Grand Staircase Escalante National Monument appears to be "carved in stone" and indestructible, in truth, it is easily impacted by human error or ignorance. In a landscape so unique, so specialized, everything is connected for its survival. Everything has a purpose, everything has a place.

"This land is alive," say the tribal peoples. And so it is.

"It gets into your blood," say the descendants of pioneers. And so it does.

We humans are changed by our relationship with the land. The land is changed by what we bring to it. When we recognize our privileged place in this ages-old dynamic, we honor it. In doing so, we honor ourselves... and the generations yet to come

SUGGESTED READING

CHESHER, GREER K. *Heart of the Desert Wild.* Bryce Canyon, Utah: Bryce Canyon Natural History Association, 2000.

CRAMPTON, C. GREGOR. *Standing Up Country.* Tucson, Arizona: Rio Nuevo Publishers, 2000.

FAGAN, DAMIAN. *Canyon Country Wildflowers.* Helena, Montana: Falcon Publishing Company in association with the Canyonlands Natural History Association, 1998.

Overleaf: Autumn is the most stunning time of year in the Escalante Canyons.

Gnarled juniper roots embrace a profusion of magenta four o'clocks in late spring. The two are often found growing in the same sandy, well-drained area.

This fledgling red-tailed hawk is probably just learning to hunt effectively. Rabbits, rodents, lizards, even snakes – beware!

Native to the new world – and still respected by hunters for their wily cunning – wild turkeys were used extensively by Ancient Puebloans: as food, for ornamentation, and in ceremony. Flesh, feet, feathers, "beards", bones, and beaks all were used.

A Great Horned Owl nestling ventures from behind its parent's protective wing. Later, this Youngster will become a dead-eye predator. Today, he is prey.

Everything is *connected* for its SURVIVAL. Everything has A purpose. EVERYTHING has a PLACE.

This little canyon tree frog has a very big voice. His mating call sounds remarkably like that of a bighorn sheep!

Rattlesnakes coil and rattle only when threatened. They prefer protected crevices and ledges, so be careful where you put hands and feet.

Before There Was a Monument

What is the span of Humankind, when measured against the long calendar of the land? We are as transient as the slot canyon's fleeting shadows, as ephemeral as "walking rain" gliding across the desert. Yet we have left our mark.

Many of the tribes now living around the Monument's borders have their own creation traditions stating that they sprang from the ground itself and hence, were one with it from the Beginning of Time. Theirs are traditions of adapting to the demands of the land, of finding and maintaining balance with the natural world in order to survive.

Monument archaeologists find evidence dating first human occupation here to roughly 10,000 years ago. The sites they have discovered, from big game hunting Paleo Indians (8000 B.C.) through agrarian-based Puebloans (1250 A.D.), collectively represent an astounding concentration of cultural resources.

About 2000 years ago, two very distinct ancient peoples—called Virgin Anasazi and Fremont—began coexisting here, apparently with very little interaction or assimilation. The Anasazi (grouped today under the term "Ancestral Puebloans") built permanent farming settlement sites near their fields. The Fremont alternated between temporary winter hunting residences in the mountains, and summer farming camps in canyon bottoms.

Their lives—encompassing both natural and cultural environments—tantalize us from arrowhead flakes, bits of woven basketry, painted pottery

K.C. DENDOOVEN

Ancient peoples *were experts at adapting themselves to the land and its resources. This mud and stone granary was built eight hundred years ago against the protecting overhang of an enormous sandstone face, using exposed slickrock as its floor.*

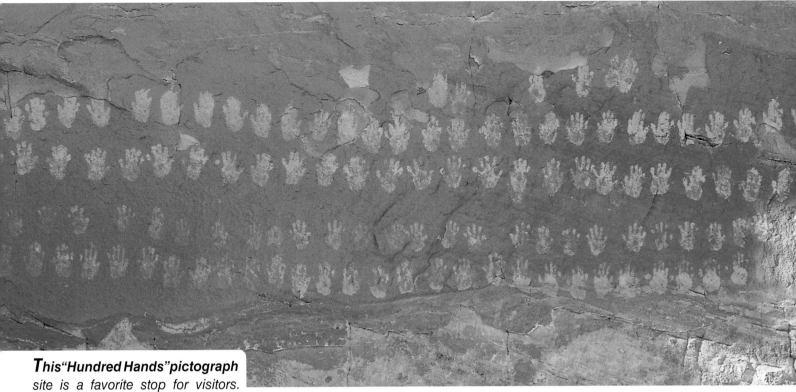

***T**his"Hundred Hands"pictograph site is a favorite stop for visitors. Clearly viewed with binoculars from the Escalante River scenic turnout on Highway 12, the rockface can also be accessed by hikers from Escalante River Bridge Trailhead. Are these individual handprints of a specific band of native peoples? Are they a tally of some kind— or perhaps a warning? Archaeologists still aren't certain of the answers.*

sherds...whisper to us from remnants of cloth, desiccated squash seeds and corn cobs, beads of traded turquoise and shell. They shout from pictographs and petroglyphs upon the rocks. They echo from daub and stone granaries, and curved kiva walls.

Scientists examine evidence of crops they cultivated, wild seeds and game they ate, how they used and manipulated raw materials. The Monument's varied landscapes, elevations, and micro-environments all demanded specific adaptations, so every detail deciphered about these ancient peoples helps us better understand how they lived here through the millennia, how and why things changed, and how their worlds and ours connect.

The region's Hopi and Zuni tribes claim cultural lineage from those Ancestral Puebloans.

Descendants of later arrivals—such as the Paiute, Ute, and Navajo—also live here. Features commonly termed "ruins"... artifacts... even certain routes and spaces traditionally or ceremonially utilized by the ancestors, are considered by today's tribes as being culturally alive and important. All are sacred. The Monument works closely with the tribes in ensuring protection of these under law, and encourages visitors to use the utmost respect when any are encountered.

CHANGING CULTURES

First historic documentations of the region's tribal peoples were recorded in the 1776-1777 diary entries of Catholic priest, Father Silvestre de Escalante. He and Father Francisco Dominguez, with their expedition of ten men, skirted Monument lands while seeking to establish a reliable route from Santa Fe missions to those in Monterey, Alta California. On their extraordinary journey around a country so raw and ragged that it would repel explorers, trappers and traders, and settlers for generations, the two padres eventually discovered all the major tributaries of the Colorado River... except the Escalante River.

That discovery, nearly a century later, officially went to fellow explorer, Almon Thompson a brother-in-law to the famed government surveyor, cartographer and adventurer John Wesley Powell. In his 1872 report, Thompson wrote: "Believing our party to be the discoverers, we decided to call this stream in honor of Father Escalante, the old Spanish explorer...and the country which it drains, Escalante Basin."

The priest's name was affixed to a region he never trod. But the name stuck. When Church of Jesus Christ of Latter Day Saints (LDS) President Brigham Young directed Mormon pioneers from

Cottonwood Canyon Road snakes through the upper end of the Cockscomb south of Grosvenor Arch. This dirt road was constructed in the 1960's in conjunction with the power line that brought electricity north to the small communities of Bryce Valley. Now, it allows vehicle access through the interior of the Monument to northern gateway towns of Cannonville, Tropic, Henrieville, Escalante, and Boulder.

Kanab and Panguitch to settle the inland area in 1875, Thompson (who was then mapping and surveying on the Kaiparowits Plateau) suggested they keep the Escalante name, which they did.

Some traditional tribal place-names were adopted by the white settlers: Kaiparowits, Skutumpah, Kaibab, Paunsaugunt. Others were Anglicized: Kanab, for instance, from the Paiute *Ka-nav*, place where the willows grow.

Still others—the majority—were discarded, and renamed to reflect the new residents and their culture: No Man's Mesa, Carcass Canyon, Dance Hall Rock, and Brigham Plains.

The new residents forged their own relationship with the land. Wide open spaces accommodated wide open spirits, but demanded industry and tightly knit communities for the new culture to thrive. Farming, livestock raising, bee keeping, mining, milling: the settlers' shared religion provided the impetus to succeed when the land resisted.

One of their legendary epics involves the San Juan Mission sent forth by Brigham Young in 1879. In a frigid November, two hundred fifty Mormon

Forty miles southeast of Escalante along Hole-In-The-Rock road, the rounded monolith of "Dance Hall Rock" dominates the landscape. While the Hole-In-Rock trail was being forged, pioneers camped at Fortymile Spring, holding their meetings and dances in the shelter of this impressive natural stage.

men, women and children set out from Cedar City across (now) Monument lands with eighty wagons trailing over a thousand head of livestock. Their "call" was to colonize the Montezuma Creek area of the Utah-Colorado border, arriving there in time to prepare fields for spring planting.

All proceeded reasonably well until they dead-ended at a cliff overlooking the Colorado River, a sheer 2,000-foot drop (600 meters) below the cleft where the pioneers stood. What were their choices? Go back the way they had come? Snow now blocked the way.

Stay? No, their mission was to push ahead. But how?

There was only one option. They would have to dig a road down to the river. Six weeks of blasting and back-breaking pick work finally produced a precipitous passageway to the bottom. In some places, the grade dropped 25 percent; in others, 45 percent! Through the "hole in the rock" notch, these pioneers lowered their wagons, their wives, their children and goods. Muscle-power—human, horse, and ox—triumphed. With only rope brakes on the wagons, they inched their way down the rockface to the river. Then once ferried across, they began again... digging and toiling their way up the other side.

They didn't arrive at the site of present-day Bluff until April—not their appointed destination, and not in time for spring planting. Yet, they had challenged an unyielding landscape, and won.

Hole-In-The-Rock Road across the eastern portion of the Monument follows their original route.

LOVE AFFAIR WITH THE LAND OF MANY VIEW POINTS

For over a century, painters and poets, musicians and mystics, master writers, and movie makers have attempted to capture the ultimately indescribable majesty and power of this place. Zane Grey's affinity with Fifty Mile Mountain is unmistakable in his book, *Wild Horse Mesa*. Architect Mary Colter mimicked Monument lands' ruins and rockfaces in her famous public building designs across the West. Artist Maynard Dixon painted them for decades and chose to be buried in nearby Mt. Carmel. President Theodore Roosevelt repeatedly enjoyed the region's wild game hunting, and never failed to exclaim about the land's extraordinary character.

This *VAST* rugged and *REMOTE* land is of national and global SIGNIFICANCE

"It sure has wore out one heck of a lot of good farmers."
That's what one former resident of old Pahreah townsite – now abandoned – had to say about the land surrounding multi-colored Gingham Skirts Butte.

LIN ALDER

***T*he Monument** is a working landscape. Traditional uses still take place in certain areas here, including livestock ranching —a testament to the cowboy culture that was introduced by Mormon settlers over a century ago. All users of Monument lands are its stewards.

Autumn light sweeps over Boulder's pasturelands, accentuating the calming solitude fostered by geographic isolation. Long Canyon waits to welcome you in one direction, the Hogback and Calf Creek Falls in the other. Here, self-reliance and independence of spirit are prized, but so are teamwork and pulling together. In some ways, stepping into the Monument's gateway communities is like stepping back in time....stripping away the nonessential, and seeing with clear vision what the future could be.

President Bill Clinton followed Teddy Roosevelt's "national treasures" lead when he declared the Grand Staircase-Escalante region a National Monument in 1996, under the Antiquities Act. "This vast, rugged, and remote land is an unspoiled frontier embracing a spectacular array of scientific and historic resources... of national and global significance," he said. This sentiment was echoed when the Monument was designated part of BLM's prestigious National Landscape Conservation System in 2001.

From ancient puebloans, pioneers and explorers, to Presidents, scientists, movie stars and visitors, many have fallen under the seductive spell of this land, and have become part of its magic. You will, too.

SUGGESTED READING

BAHTI, TOM and BAHTI, MARK. *Southwest Indians.* Las Vegas, Nevada: KC Publications, Inc., 1997.

MARTINEAU, LAVAN. *The Rocks Begin to Speak.* Las Vegas, Nevada: KC Publications, Inc., 1973.

MARTINEAU, LAVAN. *The Southern Paiutes: Legend, Lore, Language and Lineage.* Las Vegas, Nevada: KC Publications, Inc., 1992.

ROUNDY, JERRY C. *"Advised Them To Call The Place Escalante".* Springville, Utah: Art City Publishing, 2000.

*The shortest route between two points
on a map may not be the safest. There is
no substitute for up-to-the-minute,
first-hand knowledge of the area.*

Land of Many Faces, Many Uses

"Land of the *Sleeping Rainbows".That's what some early tribal peoples called these beautifully banded slumps. Near the Paria River, Chinle shale erodes into inhospitable soils whose chemical compositions discourage most plant growth, so the banding remains in clear view.*

JACK DYKINGA

The Bureau of Land Management's mandate from Congress specifically calls for multiple uses of its public lands, including those of Grand Staircase National Monument. This "multiple use mandate" is one of the primary differences between the Monument and National Parks. Many of the settlers' traditional uses of the land are still accommodated here, and may be encountered by visitors during their stay.

Approximately 12,000 head of domestic livestock graze on Monument lands. The Monument also supports a working oil field with five producing oil wells; as well as active mining claims, and sand and gravel pits.

There are nearly 1,000 miles (1,600 kilometers) of open roads within its boundaries, many of which are open to OHV/ATV travel. Rights-of-way are granted for roads, powerlines, pipelines, and other purposes.

Maintaining balance between "grandfathered" uses, recreational opportunities, and scientific study, is no small undertaking. BLM's challenge—and responsibility—is managing the Monument to accommodate human presence without losing its largely unmodified frontier character.

Named for National Geographic Society founder Gilbert Grosvenor, this rare free-standing double arch soars from the border between the Grand Staircase and the Kaiparowits Plateau. The Monument is divided into management zones ranging from extremely limited access to universal access. This system allows every visitor individualized opportunities to experience some of the landscape's most unique and compelling features. Grosvenor Arch is universally accessible with paved hiking trail and picnic area.

LIVING THE LEGEND

I"In wildness is the preservation of the world," concluded Henry David Thoreau from his Walden Pond, Massachusetts, seclusion a century and a half ago. Thoreau never laid eyes on Grand Staircase-Escalante National Monument, but he had uncovered a universal truth: wildness reminds us of who we are, where we fit, how we are connected. Cowboy and cliff-climber alike measure themselves against the same yardsticks here: wildness of landscape and wildness of spirit.

In a world hyper-stimulated by noise and technological gadgetry, the Monument offers silence, self-reliance, self-discovery. Here, you can live the legends: darkness so thick and deep, it enfolds you like a mother's blanketing embrace... silence so profound, you can hear your blood singing through your veins... beauty so shocking, so breathtaking, you have to remind yourself to breathe.

Perhaps the same forces that strip this land to its most elemental are working on us, too, as we leave the artificial world behind. Whether exploring, birding, painting, backpacking—or simply being— you find yourself slowing down here, becoming more deliberate. Noticing more. Appreciating more. Missing "the Outside" less and less.

Old-timers say once you allow this untamed country inside your heart, you will never again be able to stay away for long. Truth or legend? Judge for yourself.

P. ANDERSON

this Land's
unforgiving
NATURE
is
Legendary

Monument boundary signs incorporate a landscape blockprint design reminiscent of those created by local legend Everett Ruess. "[This place] seems like the rim of the world," wrote this poet, artist, and avid wanderer in 1934...just before he disappeared forever into the Escalante Canyons.

EXPECT THE UNEXPECTED

Exploring Grand Staircase-Escalante National Monument is an unforgettable adventure, whether it is experienced by foot, horseback, mountain bike, off-highway vehicle, or automobile. However, adventure can quickly turn to disaster—even death—if visitors are unprepared for equipment breakdowns or sudden changes of weather. This land's unforgiving nature is legendary. It is essential that accurate, up-to-date information be obtained about road and trail conditions, water access, destination accessibility and degree of difficulty before venturing into the Monument's interior.

State Highways 12 and 89 are the only paved, maintained highways that cross Monument boundaries. All roads inside the Monument, except for portions of the Burr Trail Road and the Johnson Canyon Road, are unpaved dirt or gravel. Some are maintained intermittently from late spring through fall, but even these can be deeply eroded, sand-drift-

The road that was passable yesterday might be quite the opposite today. Flash floods are well named, for they can appear "in a flash", even when the storms that spawn them occur miles away. Roiling, debris-choked waters seek paths of least resistance en route to lower ground, often churning over dirt roadways or tearing them out altogether.

ed, or extremely rocky. High-clearance, four-wheel drive vehicles are most reliable for interior travel, even in the best of weather.

Bad weather can leave any dirt or gravel road completely impassable, sometimes for several days. Skutumpah, Cottonwood Canyon, Smoky Mountain, Hole-in-the-Rock, and the Paria townsite roads include sections of clay surface which become extremely slick and treacherous when wet. It is best that visitors carry extra clothing, food, and water on all outings—in every season—and be well versed in emergency procedures.

Cell phone service and in-vehicle navigation systems are not reliable within the Monument. The shortest route between two points on a map may not be the safest. There is no substitute for up-to-the-minute, first-hand knowledge of the area, so check in with a BLM office or visitor center before beginning your adventure. Let someone know your planned destination and time of return. Once underway, expect the unexpected.

If, during any visit, you discover a site of concern or come upon something of possible scientific interest, leave everything as you find it to preserve the overall context. Then, contact a BLM office as soon as possible with a detailed description and the location.

Don't forget to look at the formations at your feet. Slickrock erosion can be an art form. Abrasive sandstone, however, punishes missteps with skinned elbows, shins, and knees.

Though these features are "carved in stone", they are not necessarily rock-solid. This multi-ton capstone may perch atop the hoodoo's delicate neck for another century…or it may crash down this afternoon. When you are exploring our spectacular country, keep in mind that it is an ever-changing landscape. Geology happens. And if you are in the wrong spot at the wrong time, you may find yourself caught up in the unrelenting forces of Nature. Think ahead.

How did that log get wedged so high up this slot canyon's walls? Water jammed it there ~ a rushing, roaring wall of water four times the height of any hiker, with the impact of wet cement. Every year, flash floods strand unwary visitors in dry canyons and washes. Avoid becoming a statistic. Be adventure-savvy, and live to tell your tale.

Honor those who came before by treating any cultural resources you encounter during your stay with respect and circumspection. Extremely fragile— like this petroglyph panel—these cultural sites, ceremonial spaces, and artifacts are considered "footprints of the ancestors" by their descendants.

LIN ALDER

Camping in the outback is an unforgettable experience on the Monument, and is allowed outside designated campgrounds with some restrictions. First and foremost, let a BLM office know your plans, including anticipated travel route and date of return. Second, be gentle with the land that has welcomed you. If you pack it in, pack it out. Pitch your camp away from water sources and riparian areas.... and away from cryptobiotic soils. Leave no trace of your passing behind except the legacy of an unspoiled landscape for those who will follow in your footsteps.

SUGGESTED READING

ALLEN, DIANNE and FREDERICK, LARRY. *in pictures Arches and Canyonlands: The Continuing Story.* Las Vegas, Nevada: KC Publications, Inc., 1993.

BEZY, JOHN. *Bryce Canyon: The Story Behind the Scenery.* Las Vegas, Nevada: KC Publications, Inc., 2002.

EVERHART, RONALD E. *Glen Canyon-Lake Powell: The Story Behind the Scenery.* Las Vegas, Nevada: KC Publications, Inc., 1998.

OLSON, VIRGIL J. and OLSON, HELEN. *Capitol Reef: The Story Behind the Scenery.* Las Vegas, Nevada: KC Publications, Inc., Rev. 1990.

RUSSELL, TERRY and RUSSELL, RENNY. *On the Loose.* Salt Lake City, Utah: Gibbs-Smith Publisher, 2001 (reprint).

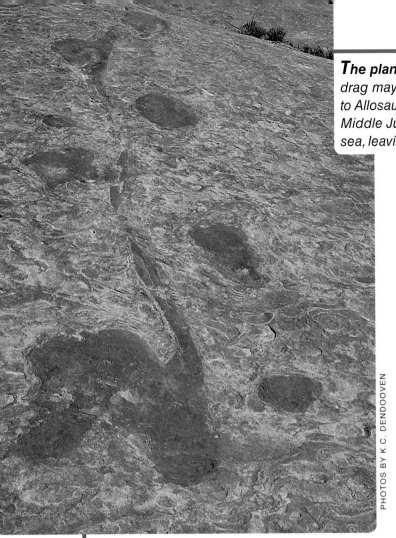

The plant-eating Sauropod that made these footprints and tail-drag may have been stalked by a big, three-toed meat eater similar to Allosaurus. Both dinosaurs—and others—crisscrossed here in Middle Jurassic times when it was the shore of an ancient sea, leaving impressions behind.

PHOTOS BY K.C. DENDOOVEN

The Story Behind the Science

The BLM actively engages partners and welcomes volunteers in many of its programs. Schools and universities, tribes, national organizations, sportsmen's groups, historical societies, even NASA—all sorts of interested public land stakeholders are encouraged to "partner up." All that is required is enthusiastic appreciation of public lands, and dedication to the conservation and wise use of their resources.

From monitoring native grasses, trees and wildlife, to counting migratory birds or constructing rain catchments... from testing stream pollution levels, to transcribing oral histories or helping excavate archaeological and paleontological sites, trained volunteers gain hands-on knowledge—and do valuable work—in the "story behind the science" here.

Articulated tail vertebrae and unusual, fossilized tendons of a young Parasaurolophus emerge from Cretaceous rock to give paleontologists clues to the life—and death—of this Crested Hadrosaur.

SCIENTIST FOR A DAY

Our government vehicle bucked and bounced over miles of backroads when we volunteers accompanied the Monument's paleontologist to a newly-discovered fossil site. "Welcome to Paleo-Central," he grinned as he swept his hand across the Kaiparowits Plateau.

We tumbled out of the rig; grabbed notebooks, cameras, tools, and extra water; then started climbing. Up. Straight up. To what—75 million years ago—had been the earth's surface. There was no apparent trail, just layer upon layer of ever-shifting, ankle-twisting rock. But our leader knew exactly where he was headed.

At long last, we stopped. "There," he pointed.

We strained to discern what seemed so obvious to his professional eye: a jumble of bone-bearing rocks crumbling out of a tree's exposed root ball.

"Trees sometimes grow on top of fossilized remains," the paleontologist explained. "Their roots feed on the mineralization."

K.C. DENDOOVEN

***T**his exceptionally rare set* *of dinosaur skin impressions has just been excavated from the discovery site. Clearly visible are two very distinct patterns of skin. Two other patterns are obscured by shadows. Many of the bones were broken before becoming fossilized inside this carcass "bag" or "mummy". This Non-Crested Hadrosaur's skull, though—found nearby—is the most complete dinosaur skull discovered on the Monument thus far.*

Time, wind, and water had laid the root ball bare. Now, the same erosion that had uncovered these ancient marvels was threatening to carry them into oblivion.

It seemed ironic that after millions of years, we suddenly should have to race against time to preserve them.

Meticulously, we took notes, drew diagrams, photographed. Our leader set to work on the jumble with his spade and brushes. A few of us followed suit, as we had been taught. Loose rock and soil fell away. More and more bones were exposed as the hours passed. Then, abruptly, we spied a pockmarked surface—as if someone had repeatedly pressed a pencil's eraser in clay.

All work stopped.

The scientist studied the pattern intently.

Brushed a little more. Studied it again. Finally, "It's skin! Dinosaur skin!" Dinosaur skin impressions—one of the rarest types of fossils.

"Wow," we all breathed together in one hushed voice. Then we cheered.

More and more skin impressions came to light under the paleontologist's brush, until they appeared to form some kind of bag around the fossilized bones.

"We may have a dino 'mummy' here," he told us, trying to keep his excitement in check and failing. "We'll need to bring in a team of professionals right away to extricate it... do more site analysis, and get this big guy back to the lab for study. Every detail can tell us volumes."

The journey of discovery and knowledge had just begun.

Cottonwoods follow Boulder Creek, carving through the Escalante Canyons. It is water that has most shaped this territory's landscape. Ancient seas and lush, moisture-loving vegetations have now given way to a land of stone. Yet, it is water that continues to give it life: snow-melt from high mountains and plateaus, deep-canyon streams and pour-offs, springs and seeps following the sandstone ledges, tiny tinajas dotting the slickrock. Whether from flash floods' spectacular inundations, or plant shadows' barely perceptible condensation, every drop of water here is precious. Every drop carries infinite potential.

All About Grand Staircase — Escalante National Monument

Grand Staircase— Escalante Partners

This non-profit Friends group was established to actively support the Monument's scientific, historic, recreational, educational, and interpretive programs and activities. By acting as ambassadors—and by fostering collaboration among volunteers, communities, natural history associations, and educational institutions—Grand Staircase-Escalante Partners strives to expand and enrich the public's experiences while visiting the Monument.

BLM's multiple use mandate translates into many types of activities being accommodated on Monument lands and resources. Visitors may encounter domestic livestock in certain areas, or recreational all-terrain vehicles in others. Not all uses are allowed in every location or in every season, however, so check current regulations for your desired activity.

Some destinations and activities (such as overnight camping) require use permits. These permits help regulate human impact on the land, and help ensure visitor safety. They—along with maps and other necessary information— can be obtained at BLM visitor centers and offices.

Contact Information

Grand Staircase – Escalante National Monument

1. Kanab Visitor Center
(Theme: Archaeology / Geology)
745 East Highway 89
Kanab, Utah 84741
(435) 644-4680

2. Big Water Visitor Center
(Theme: Paleontology)
100 Upper Revolution Way
Big Water, Utah 84741
(435) 675-3200

3. Cannonville Visitor Center
(Theme: History and Landscape)
10 Center Street
Cannonville, Utah 84718
(435) 679-8981

4. Escalante Visitor Center & Interagency Office
(Theme: Ecology)
755 West Main
Escalante, Utah 84726
(435) 826-5499

5. Anasazi State Park
P.O. Box 1429
Boulder, Utah 84716
(435) 335-7382

6. Monument Headquarters Office
190 E. Center Street
Kanab, Utah 84741
(435) 644-4300
Grand Staircase-Escalante
National Monument website:
www.ut.blm.gov / monument

H

Humankind has been in awe of this country since the beginning: its dramatic topography, its remote and nearly-incomprehensible vastness, its abundance of strange and intriguing remnants from the Time Before Man. Legends grew to describe and explain it. Songs and ceremonies carried the stories forward. Petroglyphs. Pictographs. Then, "paper words" recorded by explorers...settlers...poets and dreamers. Now, scientists and administrators have joined this honorable tradition, along with visitors and those who make their homes around Monument boundaries. The land is the constant which brings us all together. The land gives us kinship with one another, and – if we pay attention – with it. "To see a world in a grain of sand..." wrote mystic William Blake in England nearly two hundred years ago. If Blake had seen this country, he might well have enlarged his vision to include the Universe -- without and within -- as mirrored in Grand Staircase Escalante National Monument.

Looking like the paws of a *great natural Sphinx, these starkly banded cliffs and massive butte in the Paria River drainage likewise hold many mysteries. Who will unlock their secrets?*

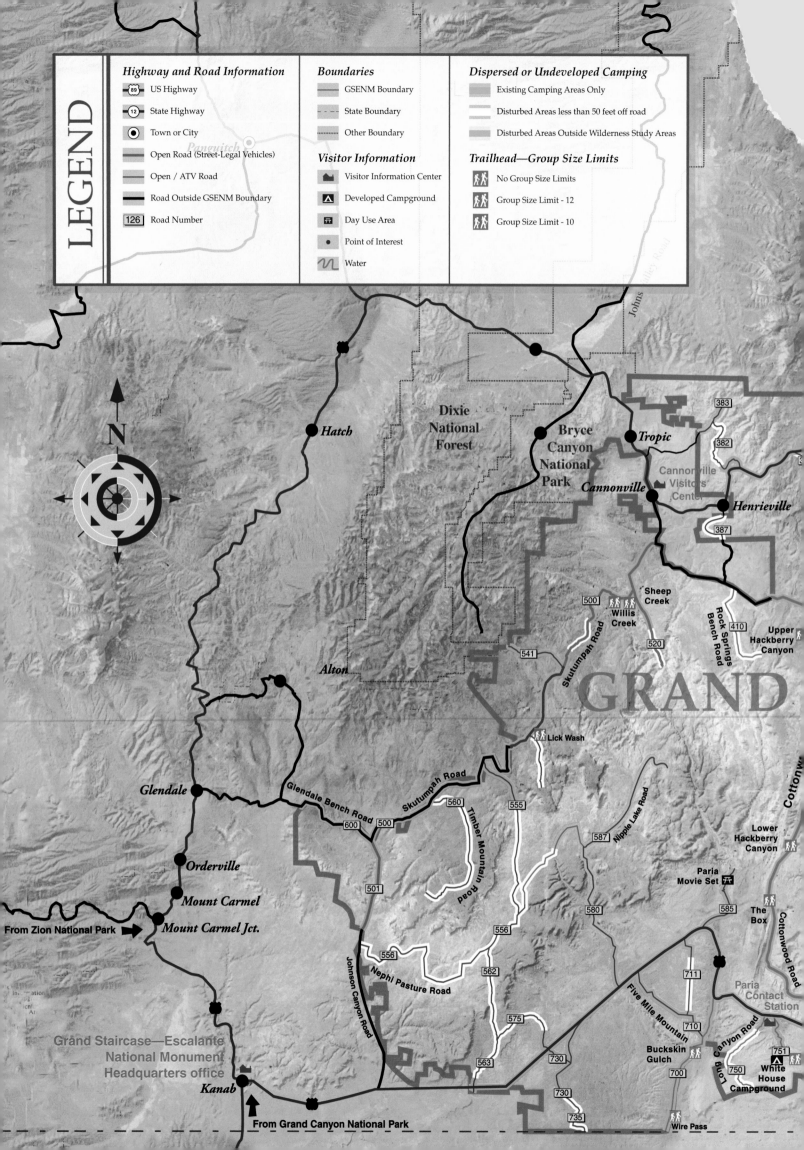

LEGEND

Highway and Road Information
- **89** US Highway
- **12** State Highway
- ◉ Town or City
- Open Road (Street-Legal Vehicles)
- Open / ATV Road
- Road Outside GSENM Boundary
- **126** Road Number

Boundaries
- GSENM Boundary
- State Boundary
- Other Boundary

Visitor Information
- Visitor Information Center
- Developed Campground
- Day Use Area
- Point of Interest
- Water

Dispersed or Undeveloped Camping
- Existing Camping Areas Only
- Disturbed Areas less than 50 feet off road
- Disturbed Areas Outside Wilderness Study Areas

Trailhead—Group Size Limits
- No Group Size Limits
- Group Size Limit - 12
- Group Size Limit - 10

N

Panguitch

Hatch

Dixie National Forest

Bryce Canyon National Park

Tropic

383

382

Cannonville Visitors Center

Cannonville

Henrieville

387

Sheep Creek

500 Willis Creek

Rock Springs Bench Road

410

Upper Hackberry Canyon

520

541

Alton

GRAND

Skutumpah Road

Lick Wash

Glendale

Glendale Bench Road

Skutumpah Road

560

555

Timber Mountain Road

587 Nipple Lake Road

Lower Hackberry Canyon

Paria Movie Set

Orderville

600 500

501

580

585

The Box

Mount Carmel

Mount Carmel Jct.

From Zion National Park →

556

Nephi Pasture Road

562

556

575

Johnson Canyon Road

Five Mile Mountain

711

Paria Contact Station

710

Cottonwood Road

Grand Staircase—Escalante National Monument Headquarters office

Kanab

↑ From Grand Canyon National Park

563

730

Buckskin Gulch

Long Canyon Road

700

751

White House Campground

750

730

735

Wire Pass

Grand Staircase–Escalante, into the Futur

Land of infinite variety. Land of fascinating complexity. Land of colors and groundforms laid out like a kaleidoscope: ever changing, ever surprising, and ever exuding incomparable beauty. This is Grand Staircase-Escalante National Monument. You could spend several lifetimes here without fully exploring – or understanding – its nuances and underpinning connections. This is a national treasure of the spirit as much as of the land, a place where people of all cultures, interests, and abilities can experience awe and wonder at every turn. It is a working landscape, one that has evolved over time to accommodate varying lifestyles and cultures without losing its essentially primitive frontier qualities. The role of science in such a unique place is more than simple discovery and analysis. Studying how all the pieces fit together helps inform decisions about how best to manage this exceptional land's many resources for the benefit of the present generation. And the next. And those generations following that. The Bureau of Land Management invites you to let this amazing place get under your skin. Let it get into your blood. Let it become a part of you, and part of the legacy that—together—we will leave to the future.

Sunrise signals new opportunities and adventures on Grand Staircase-Escalante National Monument. Each day presents the potential for new and exciting discoveries.

Inside back cover:
Sinuous slot canyon narrows beckon deeper and deeper into their heart of stone.

Back cover: Ancient sand dunes, frozen in time, forming a stairway to the sky.

Created, Designed, and Published in the U.S.A.
Printed by Tien Wah Press (Pte.) Ltd, Singapore
Color Separations by United Graphic Pte. Ltd